Sonnets about Nothing

Sonnets about Nothing

Asheesh Santram

RUPA

Published by
Rupa Publications India Pvt. Ltd 2014
7/16, Ansari Road, Daryaganj
New Delhi 110002

Sales centres:
Allahabad Bengaluru Chennai
Hyderabad Jaipur Kathmandu
Kolkata Mumbai

ISBN : 978-81-291-3534-6

10 9 8 7 6 5 4 3 2 1

First impression 2014

The moral right of the author has been asserted.

Typeset in Californian FB by SŪRYA, New Delhi

Printed at Thomson Press, New Delhi

To Ashna and Abi

CONTENTS

INTRODUCTION

I do not know if I can be called a poet or not, this is my first attempt in this genre of literature, the reader will be my judge and my best critic so I will leave this to their sensibility, appreciation or criticism.

I have been a student of poetry for over thirty years now, having had the privilege of learning this art form from the best of teachers, both at St. Stephen's College and Lucknow University in the 1980s and '90s. I will not name my mentors here, since I owe each one a lot and there are so many who have contributed to whatever meagre knowledge I have of the subject.

I, in turn, have been a teacher of poetry for the past seventeen years. And I have seen generations after me studying the same poets as I did at school and college. Probably in my time too these poets were way after their time. Why would a student in modern India be bothered with the words of a poet who was writing about the Industrial Revolution and its effects on nature? How could they even identify with words written two hundred years ago? Why, even the war poems written during the First World War have no subjectivity in India today, why would today's students be bothered with them? For this reason, poetry class, I have realized, is becoming a boring, irritating, easily avoidable and despicable waste of time.

There are modern poets writing excellent works today, why can't they be included in the whole modern teaching process? One reason that I feel, from the point of view of those who decide the curriculum, is because modern poetry is hardly poetry...

Fine, there is thought, and beautiful profound thought that the modern poets convey in simple, understandable words, but I feel that it is not thought alone that makes a poem.

There are three essential ingredients to a poem, that is the dictum passed down by the great poets of the past. A poem needs to have rhyme, rhythm and thought. A good poem will have at least two of these, a great poem will have excellence in all three. That is why poets like Wordsworth, Milton, Shakespeare, Keats, Browning, Blake and Shelley are still part of the poetry curriculum in schools and colleges. Even if the thought that they conveyed is way beyond relevance.

So the 'thought' occurred to me, 'What if I were able to give a modern thought to poetry and yet retain the rhyme and rhythm of old? Will it help in making poetry appreciable in today's day and age?' I asked friends on Facebook to give me words, simple day-to-day words that meant something to them, from their lives, so I was given the 'thought'. I received more than two hundred and fifty such words—for which I am now thankful to all who gave their time to think of words for me. I have written these poems from those words alone, so what is here is the result of words that were provided to me, the thoughts of today.

I hope the readers shall find some affinity therefore to the thoughts conveyed. What I tried to do was to relate each poem to the person who gave me the word. Facebook being a young person's domain, naturally I got most responses from my own students who had just passed out of school or college. But then since they are the target of this endeavour, I hope to keep poetry as an art form alive through them.

So if a young boy who has just left school and gone to college gave me a word, 'smile', I have based the poem on his struggle to find his way in his new situation. If a young boy, recently married, who has started to climb the corporate ladder, gave me the word 'balance', the poem has been written with him in mind yet is universally applicable in today's scenario.

So the thought is modern, but I am trying to adhere to the norms of poetry set centuries ago. Each poem is a sonnet, a fourteen-line poem that has been written since the time of King David in the Old Testament of the Bible in the Book of Psalms. Each sonnet is divided into three quartets (four lines) and ending in a couplet (two lines) adding up to fourteen lines.

Each line has been written in iambic pentameter, the ten-syllable line (syllable being the division of every word into its vowel sound, so 'sonnet' is two syllables, 'saw' and 'nett'. Each line will have ten such syllables, it does not matter how many words there are, but ten syllables are a must) that is divided into five metres where one syllable is stressed and one unstressed, that is what gives rhythm to poetry. Such was the language of poetry from the time of Chaucer, writing in the 14th century, to John Donne in the 15th century, to the thirty-six plays of Shakespeare all written in iambic pentameter, to the two epic poems, 'Paradise Lost' and

'Paradise Regained' of John Milton. The Romantic poets, Wordsworth, Coleridge, Keats and many other great poets through the ages all wrote in iambic pentameter as have I.

Most of these poems have rhyme, some do not, but the couplet of every poem is in rhyme since I hope the conclusion of every thought shall leave some mark on the reader, and what better way of leaving a mark of a thought could there be but through rhyme?

Sonnets about Nothing

This is the poem that started this quest for thoughts within, written just a few days after the Deluge that swept Uttaranchal. One will remember those days around 16th June 2013, especially in North India. Incessant rain, unrelenting, even after the disaster at Badrinath had occurred. When lakhs of people were washed away, their mortal remains too never found, families destroyed, loved ones lost forever, all that remained was despair and the questions. Why? Who? For what?

It was another evening of rain when these thoughts emerged. Following a simple status update by someone on a social networking site that said, 'It is Raining!' my thought was 'We are so safe in our homes, so away from all the disaster that has just been, we will sleep peacefully tonight... And with God's grace will wake up safely too...'

But in some homes, the rains would be a dismal reminder of all the sorrow that has just been...for whom maybe, the 'rain of tears' may never stop. So this is a tribute... A memorial to the lost lives in the disaster. To whom, somehow, I personally wish to apologize... Because 16th June is my birthday.

RAIN

We sit...raindrops fall on our window sills...
All else's quiet...where does it leave us...this rain?
That wets our hearts and minds? So will it end?
Or will we wake and be rained on again?

Will there be sunlight tomorrow?...respite?
The monsoon months have gone on long enough...
Taken them already...who could have lived...
Yet it rains! Are more to go? I just ask

I miss those beautiful evenings gone by
When there was laughter and merriment, joy.
The rain has to end...sometime...but will it
Ev'r stop raining in my soul? I just ask

I feel the rain, feel the pain of each drop
Someday I so do hope the rain will stop...

The news goes on talking about wars and riots and all the bloodshed that happens, while the first poem was about water destruction, the next had to be about destruction by fire. Each destroys in their own way, but where rain brought about a natural destruction, fire is created by man. By people crazed with anger, unreasoning, unthinking anger, that only finds vent in annihilation.

The images created here are the violent images of the war of Syria, when innocents were being gunned down for no reason. News coverage had this video of a grandmother running away from a hail of bullets with her grandson squeezed to her bosom. I can only hope they survived.

Yet one cannot blame the ones shooting too, what do they know who they are shooting at? They have a task, which is to shoot, who shall die they do not know, they may be as empathetic as me to the plight, yet have a duty to perform which they do.

That is why the last lines of the poem are so enigmatic!

FIRE

Fires, thirsty fires rage in this square,
Raging as the vast mob screams out in pain.
There was life here once, just where did it go?
Where did the joy of the street vanish to?

Is it just so easy to annihilate?
Without any care, without a reason,
The bullet does not bother to ask questions
It has a mark; it meets it when it can

What happens thence is deemed as fate.
Some die, some may be maimed, others blinded
All for a cause that no one really knows
Yet fight for, since it seems the thing to do

If only earthquakes were so kind and shake
Volcanoes would quench fires that humans make

Autumn means the fall of leaves, could falling leaves bring good luck? That is what the superstition says, if you catch a falling leaf and give it to someone, then it will bring them a day of good luck.

The season with this superstition then becomes a gift of love. Imagine catching 365 of them and giving them to a loved one... Does that not become an amazing labour of love? It is an illogical effort but what a thought it conveys.

This season of autumn where everything is dying around you can still bring hope for more beautiful times ahead. So the poem in this season of death becomes a hope for new living.

AUTUMN

If just leaves this autumn knew how to fall
Fall! there is a word, do we exactly?
Know how to fall? We do have immense dreams!
Least knowing the ditch that is before us?

They say that if you catch a falling leaf
It will give you a day of luck...really?
I then wish I'd catch three six five of them
Not for me but you. But why? you may ask...

Dunno! just that the sight of falling leaves
Fills me with hope...autumn is here so it's
Clear that winter is near...and if it's so
Could the brand new year be so far behind?

Let autumn leaves fall...each a prayer for you,
And let hope remain for bright new days too!

A poem written for a young girl. Who I hope will never have to face such rage...the male ego that finds vent in violence so often. Women eternally are at the receiving end... So has it been from ages in the past...regrettably it is the same today as well...imperfect love it is... But it is real in its own imperfect way.

RAGE

The rage that I feel...is it yours or mine?
It builds within me and finds vent in you!
I do scream and shout and create a scene
And yet you are quiet! Why? I demand you.

Is it care or scare or are you just tired
So don't fight back? So many issues, yet
You remain calm, do you have no desire
When at height of rage I am, why don't you fret?

Is it for you love me more than I do?
Or is it that you do not care? hope not.
In my defense I know my rage subsides
Then we will be us again no doubt.

Let me vent it all! let my rage find voice!
Then in imperfect love we can rejoice

A tribute to my teacher, who could be any teacher who has ever taught me. In fact, in turn I am a teacher today and hope and pray that I too could influence lives the way my teachers have influenced mine. Simple words of praise these are, a simple word of gratitude.

But like every teacher, I wish to see my students in places of high esteem. When a student earns respect, a teacher feels overly respected. When they are applauded, for a teacher, the applause rings louder. Especially teachers of nursery and kindergarten; they are the ones that make the person who he or she becomes.

Though the person never ceases to learn, all through one's life a person has teachers, so it's a tribute to learning. And when that learning bears fruit, the teachers deserve the credit too that sometimes in the individual glory one forgets to do.

So pay gratitude to the one who made you who you are, the way may not be complete, you might still go far.

GRATITUDE

I come to you with heartfelt gratitude
For making me who I am...who am I?
But your reflection...but what you taught me
Is what's here, Teacher! I am what I am

Gratitude...can be just said, tribute paid
Might mean something to you or maybe not
Do you not read yourself in my every word
Am I not but a reflection of you?

A student just I am... You, my teacher
But I pride on my learning...do you too?
I have achieved enough in my own life
But in the bargain I guess so have you!

Please do pride in me, dear teacher ma'am?
For you've made me the person that I am

Written in response to a word given to me by a student, but a tribute to women in general who have the power to move on. And why women alone? to anyone who wishes to let go of the past.

One has to let go, live life in the present and have dreams of the perfect future...that is what completes us... Make the past a weapon, an experience for the challenges ahead, and fight them. And then in one's self one finds strength to fight the demons ahead. Absolution from the past to challenges of the future is what this poem is all about.

ABSOLUTION

I feel absolute right now...feel complete
The woes of the past are done...I move on!
What was...was...what is...is...henceforth...replete
No looking back at all... What's gone...is gone

Any regrets? I am so done! Who cares?
What was...was...what is...is so damn lovely
Tomorrow is a better word... I guess
Yesterday's forgotten, absolutely

I dream of stars and honours so immense
That pains of days before may recompense!
I have no time to dwell on what could be
It's over...finally my soul can be free

Let go and live with soul freeing absolution
Finding in yourself a new creation.

A word given to me by Ms Nidhi Gupta (Mrs India International Runner Up) someone who knows all about woman power... So here is a tribute to women...

We men do tend to underestimate women...underestimate their strength and all the great things they are capable of, a man only has physical strength...a woman has more strength than a man may never even begin to understand. A man is more frail emotionally...just brute strength is not enough...a woman is stronger than man can ever be...

WOMAN

Dear Woman...what can I say...you're so
The better half of me! And I am though
Incomplete without you! yet my ego!
Inhibits me! dear woman do you know?

The very world shall cease to move without you
Even I...the man...knows it...yet ignores it
In my greatness...how can I stoop to you
Woman...the half of me in plain brute strength

I slap you and hurt you and cause you pain
For I can! can you stop me? I dare you...
No way! because I am the alpha male
I forget that I'm even born of you.

Woman...you are so strong where I am not
In your frailty, may my might be fraught

Written for a dear student, who has been a caregiver to her sister, another dear student who has muscular dystrophy, an illness that with time has been attacking her muscles and has been making it more and more difficult for this young girl to even move.

I have seen both sisters fight this disease for years, seen the conviction of the one afflicted, who would refuse help and walk alone, even climb steps when she could, till the time when she should have been in a wheel chair, instead would ask her sister to drop her to class on her scooty, and then take the few steps till her desk on her own.

But this is for her sister, who has endured all that has been asked of her, waiting patiently for her sister to prove she can do it, despite her frailty, standing on the side while her sister, the afflicted, is revered and yes applauded by all for her resolve. She is undoubtedly an unsung hero, when laurels will be placed on the head of the sister for her determination against the disease, she will just be in the audience, yet all that she has given up and endured will never get mention.

That is how it is with all care givers, one has to continue to give and give and ask nothing in return. Have the patience and the resolve of doing the best one can. All they ask for is a little understanding and a little consideration for all they have endured, that shall make their service worthwhile.

ODE TO PATIENCE

Dear patience, see my very tomb
Living in your confines with no complaints
Serving, giving, enduring without
A sigh! can you do more? oh dear patience?

Living for others? Is there more to life?
Is there an end to slavery? I ask?
Life is not about losing hope you say.
So I believe and hope forever after!

And then they say patience pays! so I pray
For I have served enough and ask! I plead!
For my own life! free from this servitude
Not servitude but my labour of love.

Just realize my life and love dear patience
And set me free so it will all make sense

A young boy gave me this word, I do not really know what he had in mind when he gave it! To me a sigh becomes a breath of life, seeing something beautiful on a vacation...say...rejuvenates and makes one ready again to face life. A beautiful painting, anything that one may find delightful that one is compelled to 'sigh' in admiration.

Keats said a 'thing of beauty is a joy forever'... The sigh of seeing something beautiful becomes life, the breath of life that will fill you with years of happiness and love. So I hope the reader finds innumerable reasons to sigh in life.

SIGH

Oh! I sigh as breathe leaves me! not really
But in passion of what appeals to me.
Breathtaking sights...beautiful moments, all
Make me sigh and always I wonder why?

Is beauty so far away that I long
To see it? is not anything here for
Me to sigh for? what is a sigh I ask?
But a longing to covet and to have

I sigh and wish for all that makes me full
I covet for breathtaking views and such
Emotions that reach the peaks of passion
Oh! let me sigh and know that I'm happy

Let my sigh find voice...let the world hear!
That passion lives in the breaths of despair

Lines given to me in jest by my wife Shweta, that I converted to a prayer for our children, son being just symbolic here, just a parent's dream to see their children win through life's struggle.

As a parent one tends to be protective of one's children, and not permit them to find their own way. This poem intends to tell parents to let them go...but send the choicest blessings and wishes godspeed. May the strongest be their guides (hence all the allegories to Greek mythology).

A tribute to parents is what this intends to be and their prayers when they let go of their children into the big bad world into a future that they shall create alone.

SAIL

Sail away dear son...to a lovely world!
More lovely then now...filled with adventure
May powerful sails through the winds unfurl
And currents guide you to a bright future

May you be a sailor of life...as me
Free from all the winds yet find your own gale!
And sail away...every wave a mystery
But it may be yours to fight or to fail

And strength of the ages are yours to find
May Jason and the Argos be your guide
Ulysess itself be your very lore
And Theseus spur you like never before

Sail away dear Son, godspeed of the past
For history remains, future may not last

Written for the word given to me by my sister Sangeeta, the only image in my mind was Wordsworth with his sister Dorothy at Tintern Abbey,

The image created here is that we are on a wonderful trip together, as Wordsworth and Dorothy were. We being religious people, naturally hope for 'serenity' and the presence of Almighty with all the beauty that we experience. We travel through an ethereal place, that is heaven borne yet earthly. But still pure, untouched, eternal, we pray that we may be close to the Almighty.

It is a serene experience of a brother and sister, two hundred years after the experience of Wordsworth and Dorothy...the brother sister love lives on, in another lifetime, in another beautiful place...that this time...is one with God.

The last line is but a tribute to our mother!!

SERENITY

You and I've come to this beautiful place
There are trees, mountains and mysterious mist!
And serenity, peace and Godliness.
All fill our hearts with joy and happiness.

Serene! there's so much to be thankful for
So much that God has given us, just now
There's music playing in our every pore,
That stills the turmoil of the world below

Dear sis, I'm at peace here, the soul awakens
To be at peace with you, is something else!
May this place, this moment and this second
Be not just a memory, an experience

Serenity that we've shared now and here.
Who knows even God herself may appear.

For one who has tried and tried again yet been rejected...what is the answer?
To quit trying? No way!...it's an ugly struggle no doubt... So many people
will be there who will tell you to give up...take up something else...there will
be so many who will laugh at you...even to your face and tell you...'No way
can you achieve...best is to give up' who will you listen to?

All dreams are made up of persistence... If you dream it...you can achieve
it... But do you have the persistence to? Not many do...so here is a poem
intended to motivate...maybe there will be stumbles along the way...maybe
people will tell you to 'give up'...it's all up to you to see your dreams come
true.

PERSISTENCE

Some try, some can, some fail along the way!
Who is to say who's gonna make it?
Those with the audacity to persist...
Be the pest who does not relent and yet

Never gives up...until the task is done.
Not give up! I guess that's the secret key!
For those who can...there will be some who'll say
Leave it! you can't do it, it's but your fate.

Not to have, and some who shall laugh ha ha!
Go ahead! they say make a fool of you!
Yet give in or give out, is upto you!
Take the sniggers with the praise, don't let go

Focus on! never lose sight of the aim
Persistence then is the name of the game.

Written for a young boy who has just 'left the nest', away from the shelters of home and school...such promise the child has...but the big bad world lies ahead...what does a boy have to protect himself? His own capabilities, yes! All that he has learnt yes! But the foes are more... So then? What will protect him?...

A smile will see him through...no doubt...a smile of the confidence that he is not alone...he has all his family with him and his friends and their love...why should this young boy be afraid? Life can scare so much if we allow it to...where we come from yet is a cushion that comforts us so. And all enemies vanquished with a smile.

SMILE

I have many reasons to smile, I feel,
Family, friends and my accomplishments.
Now a new age of my life is on me
So I've new forts to conquer, yet I smile

I laugh in the face of danger, I'm brave,
Yet shudder when I'm alone, on my own,
I need your support, dear friends and loved ones
With you with me, a smile is not so hard.

Troubles may come, problems arise I know
Who cares when the one me is so many!
See their reflections in my eyes dear foes!
And face us all if you even dare

I smile for I know, that you're all with me
To take me through worst of adversity.

What is loyalty but a realization of responsibility? Will anyone be loyal if they did not feel responsible? But is loyalty really rewarded? To the loyal rewards actually have no importance... Those who are responsible rarely seek reward...for there are other accolades that usually await them which are bigger and better than all the awards and all that money can buy...so be loyal...but before that...be responsible!

LOYALTY

I have lived the word, stood by it I feel,
Done what was demanded...did all that was
Expected, been loyal to my efforts,
Yet I receive no appreciation.

Is it fair? I ask, will my loyalty
Not receive any gratitude? and then...
Does it matter? I've been true to my task
I've done my bit, my God knows, that I have

Loyalty and responsibility
Have been met in me and I have done all
To play my part in the circle of life.
It's not over, the circle continues

Loyalty's end can never really be,
When there's no end to responsibility

Young kids may face this every day...they have so many questions that we adults fail to answer... They ask on...we continue to shun them... Is it fair? If you don't know the answer...pass it on...who says you must know everything...yet why do we stump the question? The young seek the advice of the mature... But sometimes the question becomes too difficult for the elder to answer so in their defense the young are shunned away...

The young feel the frustration of being misunderstood and lose faith. Such a sad thing to happen is it not? Elders have an important task therefore to reach out to them and help them find themselves...that is the responsibility of the mature generation... Not to leave them in a lurch rather help the young ones to find their way...no matter how weird the question...it is up to us elders to find the answer...that is what will save the generation next!

MISUNDERSTOOD

I am now a grown up...am I not? I know
Where the sun comes out from and where it sets...
I have my own theories about it all...
Who's there to listen to my point of view?

They say that I am a rebel, am I
Really? and have I not lived by their rules
Is this not my time? make my own queries
I've now enough questions about it all.

If I ask...will you answer? or will I
Still be shunned away as the kid I was
I now need to know...tell me if you can
Or shut up! I can find my own answers

Love me as I am... I pray... I'm curious
Misunderstood for sure... not rebellious

The motto of Wilsonia (the school where I studied and now am a teacher) is 'Let Your Light Shine', words drilled deep into the very being of all students. While to some it might mean everything, to others it may mean nothing at all. But that does not matter. The poem is what a teacher hopes will be the experience of an Old Wilsonian, when they leave school and find their way through various walks of life, people realize their potential that boosts them forward.

It is the shine of learning, of discipline, of determination, of devotion and dedication, that the motto does propound, (taken from Gospel according to St Matthew, Chapter 5 Verse 16). It is the answer to one's dreams if one realizes one's own light and lets it shine.

SHINE

We were taught... 'Let your light shine' so we did
We ever sparkled in school and henceforth...
And life was bright for a while, we had it all!
Then real life came upon us...the shine went...

Where did it all go?...was I lied to? was it
Just school kids fantasy created by
Exuberant teachers who knew no more
Than school's safe confines and not the real world?

And then promotions happened, I was there
In the chosen few, and higher somehow
Why? my bosses said, that they saw a light!
Somewhere the spark remained ev'n when I had dimmed

Let your light shine oh you young friends of mine
That dreams, you dreamt, will all one day be thine

Someone gave me the word...there were two thoughts that emerged...one the song from the seventies... R.E.S.P.E.C.T and another was an episode that I witnessed when in college, there was an informal discussion group that usually invited some dignitary for an enlightened discussion and the new principal in our college was invited to give us a talk at the discussion group.

During it someone asked him the question...'How will you ensure you are respected?' It was actually a very silly, undermining sort of question, but he being a gentleman just laughed it off without taking offence. He said he couldn't...'unless I hold a candle to my head'...

It was said in jest...yet a thought...respect means light... Attune to say a halo round ones head. Some may have it some may not...we don't need to 'hold the candle'...respect may light up those who deserve it. That enlightening is what the poem hopes to do.

RESPECT

There was an old song I heard in passing
Regarding R.E.S.P.E.C.T
It had a few points worth considering
The rest I have to delve on, so I'll see

Someone said to me once, you can't hold
A candle to your 'haloed' head and expect
People to respect you, so I don't
And I don't even bother with respect

I bother with love yes and cherishment
I bother with laughter and amusement
I would rather be the Clown than the King
Respect me for joy that I may bring

Respect will come if I live a good one
No candles needed then, no praises sung.

The first of the sonnets of opposites, two conflicting, opposite thoughts, hope and despair, that resonate together. Where the first hope is the positive thought, that gives positive vibes.

Que Sera Sera is a wonderful song of the '60s that consoles one, do not fear fate, 'what will be will be'. I feel a defeatist point of view, why believe in fate when there is more one can believe in?

The image created is of water, raining down from above, and as a reminder of God's promise, a rainbow appears, that symbolizes eternal hope.

The rest of the thoughts are spontaneous feelings for the word, may mean something to someone, others may disagree completely. It is a belief that lives in a dismal world that I feel keeps me going. The belief is not in a divine providence but in self, the faith is within the belief rather than without. That is where the rainbows emerge from and hope resides.

HOPE

Can I hope for rainbows? or will they sing?
Que sera sera? what will be will be?
Is hope wasted on fate? or can it bring,
Sparkling rainbows? I hope sincerely

Hope and belief...different from each other
Live in different states of mind, do they not?
One! A weak sense of longing, the other
A conviction of I'll have what I want

I will not hope, would rather believe
That I shall receive all that I hope for
Maybe not tomorrow, may be in years
But belief never gives up...it endures

I believe that my hopes shall be fulfilled
Conviction that my faith has so instilled!

Again the parallels run, water and fire. Interestingly, fire is the light that makes the candle shine, it is also the raging fire of the explosion, the fire that makes the bullet leave for its mark. There is fire in light and fire that brings darkness too.

Yet it is upto the reader to see this as a poem of hope or despair. Do you believe in the promises given to you of salvation? Do you have the 'faith' that tells you all will be well? Even if death comes to you in this time of violence, could there be peace as prophesied? Would you rather live with hope, or give yourself over to despair? It is up to the reader to decide what this poem means to the reader. Think about it...

DESPAIR

Gunning down all hope, the fire rages on,
We live in the fiery state of peril
Blasted lives, blasted from hate if not the gun.
Where once life lived, and love did dwell

Amidst the anarchy is there a voice of calm?
That can still preserve us from all harm
Or are we lost? in this rain of smoke and heat
Will no help be? And we no salvation meet?

In our grave we wait for resurrection
That is our path, our only direction
Hoping beyond hope for life ever after
That this bloodiness will pass thereafter

Face this damning slaughter, if you do dare
To live in hope amidst all despair

Call it karma, call it duty, call it destiny, we all have our paths in life, the way we have to go, the tasks that are ours alone to fulfill. The reference in the poem is to the scene from the Mahabharat as is obvious, the other is the enlightenment of Lord Buddha...two contrasting karmas that have led the persons to immortality in their own ways.

So should our goals be too, to find our own calling and achieve our goals, no matter how difficult the path may be. Yet to perform our own karma, with dedication and loyalty, with no thought of the fruits of the karma but rather enjoy the path towards its completion.

Find your karma and live it... That is all that really matters in the end.

KARMA

They stood together on the battlefield
One soldier dreading the thought that loved ones
Would die...yet Karma had to be performed
Some would succumb, others live eternally

He sat and meditated, he found it
In a flash, it was clear, and he taught it
To those who heard, would take it on, their deeds
Would meet it...when it was done and accounted

I am doing mine, but in my own way
Finding my path to immortality
The way is mine and the aim mine too
Reach it I will, at my speed...at my will

The Karma's promise, that I've made to me
Finding sense in all life's ambiguity

Fiddler on the Roof is a classical musical of the 1970s that told the story of Jews suffering during the Russian Revolution, at the very start of the 20th century. How the Jews living in Russia in 1910 or so, under the Tsar, were trying to maintain their religion in a hostile environment.

Those living the corporate lives today suffer a similar situation as the 'Fiddler on the Roof', who has to play a 'simple tune' while maintaining one's balance. The simple tune being the simple needs of life, home, family, basic amenities of today, but corporate life becomes more difficult all the time, but the fighter fights on to maintain the balance. Not with 'tradition' that kept the Jews going in Russia, but the fear that what would happen to their lives if they ever stopped.

I do not intend to satirize the struggle but do intend to convey that 'stop fearing'. There is a way out for them who wish to get out of the circus. The balance of life never stumbles, it always remains. Life has an uncanny way of looking after itself, if only one believed.

BALANCE

Precariously we step, finding a pace
One too fast or a sudden move...we're gone
They throw balls to juggle too and say 'race'
That's how life in today's mad world goes on.

The Fiddler had balance with tradition
That was lost by years of revolution
So how do we stay put on the tight rope
What do we have? and for what can we grope?

Fear! Dastardly fear is our biggest friend
Fear of looking down, down the valley's deep
A fall takes you low, to the very end
Just stay on, move on, juggle on, you creep!

That's our tradition it's all that makes sense
We'll fail it all if we lose our balance

Another depressing image of metro life, to be caught in traffic on a panic-filled day, or at the end of a day when one wishes to be home, yet is surrounded by the multitude of humanity that lives an equally tension-filled life and is stuck in the same situation. Here is a poem of tension release.

Just forget it all, for a minute, in the deepest moments of despair, just find an escape to one's 'happy place', and what better way to find a happy place than one's memories.

But then the mind is an amazing mechanism. Maybe some dreamed-of future event or something one looks forward too could be one's happy place. Hence, just leave the tension of the moment and heed to the voices in the mind. Very soon happiness and peace you shall find.

VOICES

You wish for silence in turmoil-filled days
Horns blaring at you at every crossroad
Shouts, snarls and angry people everywhere
Somewhere in it all there is peace...feel it!

Leave the grind, while you sit at the steering
Leave the noise, escape to a happy place
In the din, a dim sound can carry you
Away, and help to fill this noise with sound!

Voices, joyful voices from your own youth
At home, in college and school, simpler times
Voices of loved ones, voices heard rarely
But fill the soul with gladness, even now

Voices of my past, voices yet to be
Makes now peaceful as I'd wish it to be

This was a word given to me by a dear colleague, an enthusiastic young man with the determination to 'Explore', so it was my suggestion to him to go to places unexplored. We rarely look within when we are amassing our knowledge of the world around us.

The journey within is a beautiful one, one finds so much untouched potential, answers to so many questions about oneself if only we explored within. Do we need to follow a particular career? Is there more that one could do with one's life? Are the things that seem to matter so much, really important? Explore one's own mind, not to find something as big as nirvana, but a simple reason to choose another way of life, that at the end of it all could make all the difference to how one looks back at one's life, that itself could make the exploration worthwhile.

EXPLORE

These crevices in our way, do we dare?
Explore, and find the mysteries within?
Do we pass them by, in our daily care?
And miss the potentials that lie therein?

Explore artifacts, and our history
Find where we came from and where we can be,
Exploring depths of the earth, of days past
Hoping to find out who we were at last

But explore in us is a task we lose
Finding out who we are remains so bleak
Excuses galore we can always use
To remain unknown to what makes us weak

Explore within and without my dear son
Exploration then will have its deeds done!

What is genuine? A diamond stone? A really expensive watch? A thoroughbred? Does a thing being valuable make it genuine and worth cherishing or is there more to be thought of when we cherish? These are the questions this poem delves into.

Feelings associated with something that others may call fake may be equally pleasurabe. Ask a child how he loves his toy spaceship? Even more than he would a real one.

The fake sometimes give so much happiness, it is not always the most expensive things that one will cherish. The trust and love for something that is fake may be even more fulfilling and joyful.

So give fake a chance...it may come in handy someday.

GENUINE

Dictates of existence usually makes
Us cherish the genuine and hate the fakes.
Agreed and understood, cannot refute
But I can't accept this as absolute

For who is to say, what's real or what's vain
Can't a beach stone be better than a gem
A mongrel more lovable than a Dane?
Isn't a toy spaceship more than real to 'them'?

Genuine is what genuine does, the 'real' call!
The joy of the 'thing' means more than its cost
In relations too reality's lost,
It's trust that matters more, and joy...that's all.

So may what's not genuine not our hearts break
Find faith and gladness in that which is fake.

A word given to me by a clever ex-student, a science scholar who I know shall do very well in life. So I took the magic of science and life to convey this thought. Science today can change lives immensely, we see it working every day. With the rapid innovations happening in every technology, medicine, construction, discovery, space...everywhere.

Finding the 'magic of science' is not enough however, but to find the way to influence lives positively...through whatever magic one has within, is another magic altogether. For that however you actually don't need to be a scientist. But for a person, with a 'Heart of Gold', that alchemy of changing hearts, with love and kindness can and will change the lives of all around. That is where alchemy actually is, the magic of changing things to gold, to change lives will then be the most magical science.

ALCHEMY

To make golden is a dream of many
To finding riches and all that it can bring
Easy paths there may be though uncanny
Unknown, eerie, evil and so damning

Alchemy is a hope of the damned weak,
Finding fortune from the easiest means
Please look for struggle and successes peak
That's where happiness is, has always been

Find alchemy in emotions, change hearts
And minds, change hate for love, and anger too
May people respect you till life departs
The magic of change will be yours to do

May I turn very hearts and minds to gold
Alchemy's most magical I am told

Another science student gave this very scientific word to something we see every day, fizz or bubbles in a glass... The poem turns this scientific term to mean something very different, as it did in the last...bubbles of life.

Simple joys of life that call for celebration, celebrated through bubbles, be it an aerated drink, or champagne. Chemistry here becomes the science of bonding rather than just science.

So live a celebrated, bubbly life, let the fizz go on...

EFFERVESCENT

It's easy to celebrate, see a glass
Little bubbles sparkling, in a chilled frame
Tells us to be happy while the fun lasts
The 'fizz' may go soon, then it's all the same

Not all moments in life could be bubbling
Not every day can be thus aerated
Realities that bring us down tumbling
And partying then gets evaporated

So cherish the chemical reaction
Of friends and nonsense, silly chatter
Old buds, with no hope...with no solution
Chemistry of which is all that matters

Life is so effervescent, bubble on
Friend in your air, may my troubles be gone

Given by someone who has lost faith in love.

Years of marriage and with too much life in between... Love tends to find a backseat when life takes over. The beautiful passion, the sighs, the heart beating, that the young think is love will pass away so soon... Love conveyed through this poem is a lifelong commitment...that will survive even though the passion may pass... There is so much one has to adjust to, so much one has to live with so that love can survive. The question therefore is...will love survive? Or will the ephemeral passion simply cease to be?

In the end...true love will survive.

LOVE

Love!... Infatuation! to find appealing
Those are not the ways of love's true call
It's a hurt causing emotion and feeling
Consuming happiness, joy, freedom and all.

Hurt!...a wise word here...in a few real hours
O lovers? once the wave of first love dies,
Hurt, pain and heartache alone will be yours
Of 'dear' love grown cold! With tears and sighs

Headiness disappears? reality
Checks my dear...that is where love really lives!
In the wrinkles and the belches and the
Anger, mistakes that you're forced to forgive

Be ready for reality! no more...
Then love will be forever to endure

Sin here is not the breaking of the commandments as talked about in the Old Testament of the Bible. Sin here is also not the two commandments of Jesus Christ from the New Testament, but it is the thought derived from Jesus' commandments. 'Love your God with all your heart' and 'Love your neighbour as yourself'.

Here sin is hurting someone, breaking someone's heart, and whose heart can a person break but one you love and who loves you. This is the worst kind of sin...but the cost of this sin is not death...it is guilt, and that guilt is worse than death itself.

Because it is easier to forgive another, but to forgive oneself is very difficult. If we can forgive ourselves, we may feel lighter, we may feel redeemed.

But the best is to never commit the sin of hurting someone you love.

SIN

Terrible word that leaves us shuddering
Shivering in our skins and wondering
Awaiting the results as on we live
For that's how we are raised...what we believe

Sin is within...not without...see it play
On our conscience as we seek redemption
That shall never come...yet we hope someday
We'll pay our debt and have absolution

We sin when we hurt loved ones...lose their trust
We sin when we lose ourselves in their eyes
to redeem is to beg forgiveness first
From them before you hope they'll not despise

Humanity of sin lasts forever
Self redemption maybe closer than ever

When I was given this word, the first thought that struck me was the egotist and altruist debate from Ayn Rand's 'The Fountainhead', how the egotist is a much more harmless person, for he lives for himself. The altruist, because he likes to give to others becomes a mean, cruel person because he demands others to return his favour in the light of his sacrifice.

St. Paul in his letters in the Bible too reiterates Christ's teaching, about a person who turns the other cheek when one hits you. Gandhi too used this tool well in fact. Think about it...how many times will such a person be hit? And by turning the other cheek... The altruist is shedding 'coals of fire' on the oppressor...isn't that astonishingly cruel?

The altruist/ the philanthropist is actually the cruel one in this way. The selfish, egotistical person then is harmless for he only cares for himself and no one else. But then he does not bother anyone else either.

So be selfish and live for you... That's the simpler way to do what you do.

PHILANTHROPY

Philanthropy! Is an awesome skill
The altruist can with goodness kill
St Paul talked of coals of fire on who dared
Hurt the one on whom kindness is ensnared

Generosity is a mean weapon
That is but ignored by the selfish one
The power of being selfless can undo
All the good that selfish men do for you

I am self-absorbed, my muse is all me
Altruism is to me a cruelty
Egoist I am, love me, it's given
Selfish deeds, by me are then forgiven

Yet I am harmless as harmless can be
Compared to the sword of philanthropy

I have heard many people say, 'I never look back... I only look forward', that is an amazing and ambitious way to live and I wish them luck. But with this word I was forced to introspect my own feelings on the subject.

I love to look back, recount all the good days gone by, the magical moments of childhood games and fun in teenage and young adult life. The cherishable times spent with loved ones... I love to revisit them. I can't let go...and why should I?

Also is the saying, those who forget history are condemned to repeat it...so how can we not constantly look back and measure the path ahead. The future maybe bright, maybe over bright if we don't tone it down with the darkness of the past.

I too look to the future but not without gripping onto the support of the times gone by.

NOSTALGIA

'I remember when', 'remember it all'.
Not many do...our history recall
It's long gone, it serves no real purpose
In life's daily grind, life's daily circus

And yet the past is real...and we lived it
It is us...but yes its gone...it's not now!
What's left's memory, it may not benefit
Us who live in the present...yet somehow!

Now wants our then, that we miss it, is clear
Days gone by and minutes, hours and ev'n years
The way we were and who we were and where
Forgetfulness is a gift for those who dare

I hope never to forget that I'm me
Nostalgia, saves me from anxiety

They say 'knowledge is power' and so it is...but here knowledge is not about power but the simple thought of making the world a better place. Yes knowledge has given us amenities, knowledge is making life simpler. But with it knowledge is also helping us to understand the world that we live in. And hopefully it will help us in making the world a better place.

A simple word...becomes a simple tribute to knowledge which I as a teacher have to love and respect and honour and preach to my students. Respect knowledge for knowledge's sake, not only what you may be able to do with it...but cherish all the knowledge that you have, because that is what makes you the person that you are.

KNOWLEDGE

Questions abound, solutions do exist
The knowing is where ignorance isn't 'bliss'
We need answers, we need to know so much
Knowing is existing, yet to feel in touch

Knowledge takes us forward, in time and space
Move on, knowing more than those gone before
No stopping, no pausing in this brutal race
Knowledge is wanting to know ever more

We have seen it all, days of not having
Of wanting and dreaming and of craving
As we grew, it all came to us, who knew?
With us too, knowledge of our world too grew

We have the say, we alone have the power
For knowledge itself makes us who we are.

The flame here is the emotion that burns within each one of us, to an extent these emotions need to be kindled to take us ahead, to help us lead a complete life, but let them not get out of control because the flame then...turns to a blaze that can burn you down.

Keep negative emotions in check, don't let them overpower you because the person who shall suffer the most by this 'unchecked fire' is you.

Keep the flame burning, 'Let there be Light', but don't let it ruin you with its blaze.

FLAME

Have you ever gazed into a fire?
It's captivating. Mesmerizing
That also happens with fiery desires
Some which just can be so hypnotizing

Passion scalds, anger singes and envy burns.
So here is a lesson that's worth the learn
When we permit our fires to shine too bright
The kindling flame turns to a blazing light

So control it, tame the flame, keep it in check
It is violent, can cause devastation
Emotions can raze to annihilation
Let not a house char down by a simple spark

May I quench the flame, without and within
Ending the burn, so the warmth may begin.

A simple thought here, a thought of innocence actually, of believing. There is so much scepticism in the world that the simple beliefs are ridiculed. Why not be free to believe if it gives one joy?

Believing is a positive innocent emotion, some of the beliefs people may find silly...accept it, but be honest here and be optimistic too.

But the most important belief that anyone should have is the belief in oneself...that one can do whatever one hopes to and dreams to. Do all that it takes to realize one's ambitions. That definitely is the most important positive belief of all.

This is however one poem that is not in iambic pentameter...it sounds more innocent and lyrical in its form as is.

BELIEVE

I believe in the spirits, I am scared of them all
I believe in the wishes of catching leaves in fall
I believe in the shooting star, darting cross the sky
I believe in God and never dare ask why

I believe them when they say that all is well
I believe in salvation of heaven after hell
I believe in the cloud in the rainless season
I believe in miracles for no abject reason

I believe there this goodness in all I perceive
I believe in salvation, in blessings I receive
I believe there is hope when all hope is naught
I believe in redemption when pain is fraught

But most of all I believe in who I am
Believing in all I hope for, in all I can.

Word given to me by my cousin Jaya at Christmas-time, during which each year I have this major issue with the whole concept of Santa Claus...where has this jolly old man come from and taken away the whole essence of this festival from the birth of the Saviour? Children of today even think that Christmas is the birthday of Santa Claus rather than Jesus Christ.

It is all a hype that has been created by toy manufacturers and card makers and Hollywood producers who need to sell their products through someone more tantalizing like Santa, rather than the real Christ.

All Christmas has become therefore is like a commercial, that intends to advertise and to sell products. Gifts, stockings, Santa, reindeers, North Pole all being symbols of this commercialization.

To render Christmas to its sanctity, these will have to be let go of, which I know is difficult. This poem just intends to make people aware of what Christmas has become, and what it really should be. Maybe in years to come, good sense and real Christmas cheer shall prevail.

CHRISTMAS

And so it's Christmas time, do you feel the cheer
Kids so wait for it, all through the year
For sleigh bells to ring and Santa's presents
Those are all that matter, all that makes sense

It's everywhere one looks, in this season
Santa, the reindeers are the sole reason
And seem the only celebration cause
Christmas has been usurped by Santa Claus

The Christ child is forgot, in Bethlehem
Left unnoticed in commercial mayhem
The Star, the Shepherds and the Three Wise Men
The Stable, the Death, have been forgotten

Christmas too needs to be resurrected,
From the 'Hallmark' world we have created

A mad sonnet, but there is 'method to my madness' as it intends to convey passion and love and craziness, and we all need a little crazy to keep us sane. A little mad passion to enjoy our everyday life. Simple things like music can be loved more if some madness is added to our emotions.

So be mad in your passion, in your love, you will definitely love better then.

MAD

I'm mad about the sunset, everyday
Mad about the music that I hear play
Mad about the poems that the greats have sung
Mad as the poets like me, unread, unsung

Mad with passion, what else is there I ask?
madness for some is an illness alas
For me I hope this illness shall remain
And passion, love, craziness I can retain

I am mad about you, it is so clear
Mad about what I long for what is dear
A moment, a time, is all that I ask
To be insane...sanity is a task

May madness know the craze of sanity
Passion found in insensibility

When I got this word, I was reminded of Coleridge's 'Frost at Midnight' when he is sitting in front of the fire and sees himself in a class room years ago, the him in the classroom sees the older self in front of the fire. A sort of a time portal, that we with all the sci-fi movies can identify with but it is amazing that Coleridge envisioned it two hundred years ago.

Memories do haunt us, but they also become our happy places that we can revisit in our minds. It is these memories, these experiences that should determine our present. The bad memories and the good together make us the person who we are. They can disturb yes, but they can soothe too, so don't let yourself be bothered by memories, learn from them, may they also give you pleasure. For your memories are you, you have made them, you must live them too.

MEMORIES

On a cold winter night, they do rush back
Like a villain plunging knives in my soul
To forget them all, I hope and yet I lack
Strength to let them go for they make me whole

Memories, of what I am, from where I've come
For I can never let go of my past
I see what I was and what I've become
The joy of my today I hope shall last

But why? why cannot I be he again
The younger me...the boy I used to be
He is here somewhere, the school boy, the same
Wondering how tomorrow's going to be

Memories of the past do haunt the now
Yet make today what it is somehow!

If only the laughter could last forever, something I try to give my children, by being their clown, always the butt of their jokes, that is what I hope I can give them always. Joy and laughter.

They are still very small, I don't know if it's the right thing to do, but we continue to try and keep the ugly side of the world as far from them as possible. We give them a sheltered life, where there is no crime, no war, no pain, no hunger, nothing evil. Instead we try to fill their little world with laughter.

Till the time they are thrust into the big bad world on their own, (I hope I can delay this till as long as possible) I hope to keep them delighted.

DELIGHTED

I am but a clown, that's all I can do
Clowning, to make you laugh I so hope to
Delight you always, wipe away your tears
Giving tears of joy instead, laughs and jeers

I delight in you no doubt, your joy warms me
When you laugh my fears subside, it calms me
For I fear that my jokes might cease to be
And sorrows again will be reality

For minutes or hours let's forget it all
The hurt and all the pain that surrounds us,
The hunger, and war and harsh deaths dire call
All the ugly real world that abounds us

So please laugh on, forget it all with me
In your free giggles let my soul be free

A word given be a dear 'simple' young boy. I felt it is an apt word, and helps me talk about the simplicity of these verses. These are very simple words, yet try to convey some deep thoughts. Find joy in the simplicity of life, why delve on complications which may just confuse? When there is so much to appreciate and make life all the more worth living.

SIMPLICITY

Simple words make rhythm and rhyme so sweet
Bead together ideas and thoughts complete
Why waste them musing in complexity?
That lead to nothing but perplexity.

In simple joys is life everlasting
The glee of which is worth contrasting
With the stress of big pleasures and desires
That the foolish, covetous heart aspires

The rain that wets a parched soul in monsoon
The mango juice running down palms in June
The warm blanket wrap on a wintry morn
The chirping of the waking birds at dawn

May we live on with pure simplicity
Safe from abject doom of complexity

The Christians believe in life everlasting... 'For God so loved the world that he gave his son, that who so ever believes in him will not perish but have life everlasting' (John Chapter 3 Verse 16). But then no one really knows for sure what will happen after we die...will we be locked up in our graves and will we continue to wait 'eternally' for the second coming?...that too is a scary thought... So here is a poem that hopes eternity shall be like a flash, coming to you the second you die and then shall lead to eternal life.

Whatever be our fate, it is a hope and prayer that all will be well in the life to come... That eternity will be in a better place than the grave.

ETERNITY

Does it exist or is it really a myth?
We hope eternity is... but is it?
Do we live with a false, unreal belief.
That helps see us through life's joy and grief

Is it just a vain promise that He made?
And died on a crucifix, and was laid
In a shallow grave, and sealed by a stone
Does He too await eternity...alone?

Three days was His eternity...believe
That's the promise...do you therefore perceive?
Eternity means, proclaims evermore?
Whereas it might be a moment no more

May a time's fraction be eternity
Rejoiced forever in the Almighty

A shy young boy gave me this word. I remember him fumbling, stuttering through a recitation competition, mumbling out unclear words and then making a mess of his whole presentation. It does happen to shy people who lack confidence.

Public speaking is among the greatest fears that a person may have, as bad as say the fear of heights. The only way to get out of shyness is by facing your fears. Maybe the next time this boy will stand and speak he will be more confident having faced his fears once.

The only way you can rid yourself of shyness is by facing your fears, confidence will automatically be delivered to you from it.

SHY

The heart palpitates, the tongue hesitates
The dizziness of the mind recreates
The terrors of the past, weird, unknown ghosts
The attempts, endeavours again are lost.

Why, why do I, try and try and try
And yet stumble just when it matters most
People say 'it's just because you're so shy,
Try some more, don't worry, all's not lost.'

Yet I try, to face the demons, to speak
To face the crowd, to not sound like a freak
To hold my own and to not be bogged down
But this shyness takes me from knight to clown

I wish my shyness would just blow away
Confidence, fortitude, would be mine to stay

Be scared of the real, not the virtual, the real scare is there within us, to be left alone, without love, without support. Ghosts etc, are hardly reason to be scared.

But one must realize that loved ones shall leave, so no matter how evasive we are of this reality, it is an inevitability. Instead of being scared and running away from it, embrace it and by so doing make the time one has with loved ones count. Be kind and gentle, don't hurt them, spend as much time with them as possible and cherish each moment.

Then when the time comes to bid farewell, it won't be that scary after all.

SCARED

Those terrible images that haunt me
Raise their ugly head and snare and taunt me
Leaving me perplexed, anxious and confused
And my very faith-filled soul lays bruised

What scares me but? Not ghosts or vampires
Not the sinking ship or the quagmire
Not my death, nor excruciating pain
Nor rejection, nor the look of disdain

But to lose what I have really does scare
The love of loved ones, the hugs of friends
The loss of them will be pain that I can't bear
And maybe that itself will be my life's end

But everyone must leave I should realize
That life itself does death epitomize

'Death be not proud' was a pretentious work of John Donne way back in the 16th century...but a work that shook the very fears of dying... This poem hopes to do the same. Death is seen in two lights here, as a release from all the struggles of life, many would welcome death from their present situations, an escapist idea no doubt, but still many might see it as a release.

The second is the cruelty of death when someone young or someone who has so much promise is snatched away. One cannot help but ask why? God's will is blamed as is the uncaring hand of death.

But then there is life that saves, life which is composed of moments that are captured as memories, life that has been lived with people who matter, filled with love and laughter and joy and happiness, kind deeds, goodness that even death cannot erase. So how can mere death take away so much? Hence death loses where life has been lived.

So live completely in what time you have, immortality is not so difficult then...and to vanquish death, the easiest task ever.

ODE TO DEATH

You are the finality, end of life
Farewell to damning struggles and the strife
You terminate all anxieties and stress
In your considerate arms fears compress

But Death you snatch away all love and care
When those we love you cruelly ensnare
For when the guiltless, meek and young do die
One cannot help but ask the reason why

But life gives memories and joys that live on
Loving moments are relived though long gone
People passed never really say good bye
Donne said 'Death be not proud' and so do I

So cherish the time that life has given
Then death's hastiness can be forgiven

This is a sonnet of a fan...a fan of the band known as Jethro Tull especially of Ian Anderson the vocalist and the flutist of the band.

Most of the sonnet is made up of titles of their songs... entwined together into a poem. The image is the band through its 'Whistler' (one of their songs) calls the listener to hear their music...it is like a dream for the fan to hear them play...they promise 'let me bring you songs from the woods' (another song) and the listener waits.

Finally the songs come pouring out, not one, not two, but all the great songs that make up the lines of the third stanza, till the listener himself becomes the songs 'the minstrel in the gallery' who is 'too old to rock and roll, too young to die.'

Jethro Tull... live long and prosper!!!

TULL CALL

The piper piped his pipe and I listened
To the sweet dream, 'Whistler' as he whistled
I waited with bated breath for the crescendo
Bated abated that lest breath stop though

But let's start again from the beginning
'Let me bring you songs from the woods" he said
So I stayed at the edge. words still ringing
Will he bring me them? what if not? I dread

It came from deep within, the awesome blast
The witch's promise, living in the past
Soulful melody, life is a long song
Thick as a brick, heavy horses, aqualung

The minstrel in the gallery am I
Too old to rock and roll, too young to die

My first of few responses to words of other poets, these are my personal thoughts, not given to me by anyone...but a response to great works of poetry I have read and admired. 'I Sit and Look Out' is a wonderful poem by Walt Whitman, written in the 1850s. Whitman talks about the sadness and anguish of the day, most of which still resonates in today's age as well.

Young boys in Whitman's day were impulsive and rash, they are so today too. Mothers and wives and girls were beaten, ill-treated and abused then, as they are today. Famines, natural calamities, holocausts, were then too and are seen today as well.

But Whitman mentioned atrocities to 'Negroes' in his work. That one word no longer exists, so much so that the nation that Whitman wrote in now has an Afro-American President. Many times has this question been asked, Whitman was a revolutionary poet, but what difference did he make? What makes his poetry be read today nearly two centuries later? The answer is his universality! His poems were important when the abolishment of slavery happened under Abraham Lincoln 150 years ago. His poetry is as important today, since even in our different age and era, maybe even with one word at a time, since 'negro' as a word is as abolished today as is slavery, the world is still changing, ever moving forward towards that distant dream of a utopian world of perfection.

I TOO SIT AND LOOK OUT

Years ago he sat as I and saw his time
The sickness, the dirt, the pain and the grime
I sit again at the self same window
Hoping not to see the same innuendo

But yet I do, the boys are still the same
Regretting when they can't surpass the blame
Women, mothers ill-treated as they were
Punishment as men of today confer

And atrocities of today exceed
The powerful ones of our now do succeed
In making the dire lots of death to be
Slights of degradation on 'Negroes' be

But, if words like 'Negro' can cease with time
World has but transformed, one word at a time

Written in response to the word given by a dear young student, a quiet boy, ever courteous and dedicated to his studies and duties as a cabinet member. Always eager to please, a boy with so much potential that I sincerely hope his dreams shall be fulfilled.

So is my advice to all, never stop dreaming, as is said often these days, 'The best dreams are seen not with your eyes closed, while you are sleeping, but with your eyes open, while you are awake.'

So make the most surreal dream real, not in your mind, but with dedicated efforts, with falls and stumbles no doubt, even with failures along the way, but dreams will take you further when all else may tell you to stop. But please don't stop, because dreams await you.

DREAMS

Awake or asleep does it matter when?
They come to you, maybe sordid or sweet
Maybe nightmarish or maybe pleasant
Or maybe where the real and unreal meet

Our lives are made up of all our dreams
Our ambitions for what we hope we'll be
Making them real isn't as easy as it seems
But believe in what you are, who you'll be

If you continue to dream, the world is yours
If you see it in your mind it is real
Touch the dream, feel its every pore
Make it possible no matter how surreal

The dream is a dream if it's in the mind
You will live it all if your dream you find

Here the readers are being asked to imagine their last breaths of life. What will be their thoughts in that moment? Will they be at peace? Ready to go onto the path that awaits them? Or will they still have unresolved matters that they now can never hope to complete.

The poem is a word of advice, to make people realize the importance of time they have. If there are 'things to do', do them now. Have yet to resolve differences with a friend or relative? Do it now. Have ambitions to realize, work on them now. Have regrets for sins committed and seek retribution, come to the Lord now. That is the only way that your distressed soul will be redeemed.

So seek the redemption today when you can. Who knows what tomorrow shall bring.

REDEMPTION

The ping in the room is continuous
The breathing of your lungs is strenuous
Any minute of the day could be your last
Death is approaching and approaching fast

What do you see? what do memories tell you?
Are you happy in that moment? at peace?
Are you prepared for the fated release?
Or are you still languishing with things to do?

Don't wait for it, do it now, don't regret
What you could do now with ease, might get hard
Don't let anything be left in your debt
Cause your time of redemption could be marred

You can have the redemption that you crave
Beg forgiveness, clear the list, before the grave

I was very young when the riots occurred in Moradabad way back in the 1980's, but can still remember the screams and cries that the night air carried through the city. It was an ugly time for the city, thankfully ever since, even when other parts of the country have seen their own share of violence, my city has not.

I know of stories during that time when neighbours refused to help neighbours, how could they help? When the very mobs were on a war path, how could they risk the lives of their own families? They shut their doors completely and tried to obliviate the very sounds that resounded in the streets. It is understandable but still, to this day animosity lives in these neighbourhoods.

Can man ever be so generous as to give one's life for another? Such stories abound too, it is upto each of us how we live. Are we the killer? Or the giver? Or the martyr?

There are three ways of living in hostility...which way will you choose?

HOSTILITY

Hostility that surrounds us does scare
It's not indifference, nor that we don't care
But raising a hand of help brings trouble
So we live in our apathetic bubble

Do you hear the war outside? it's so loud
Rather than intervene we block our ears
Living safely within our self worn shroud
We think we're safe yet die before our years

The song of pure love is within us all
If only we had the strength to sing it
A lullaby to soothe each hostile call
With harmonic peace that we could bring it

A raised hand has power, to help or to hit
To which of these ends will your hand submit?

I asked my seven-year-old son to give me a word for a poem, all he could think of was fun. It was an appropriate word for him to give, and so I wrote this sonnet for him, keeping it as simple as I could hoping he would understand it. But he is seven, that was asking too much.

Maybe someday he will, someday he too will be a father and then maybe this poem shall have more meaning for him. Because that is what this poem is all about, a father (or mother) and a son (or daughter) growing up together, learning from each other. A child learning and growing each day, a parent learning to be a better parent from their children.

Smile at the joy of innocence. Soon someday the innocent child will no longer be so have all the fun, while it lasts. Tomorrow it may not be.

FUN

You are seven, whole life awaits you son
The very race has only just begun
For you each day is and should be a quest
A journey where you never stop to rest.

You may not see it so, in your own way
You don't see it in your innocent play
You don't realize what you've learnt today
But we can see you growing, every day

And it's wonderful to see you have fun
To laugh with joy, to see you run in the sun
To skip along, to dance and to sing
You don't know the happiness your smile can bring

Have fun my dear son, may you live each day
Completely learning from your joy and play

The word given to me, late at night on Facebook, I guess the sleepless night the person was having prompted it. I remember it was a very cold January night...winters had been long and harsh in 2014 and one could not but help pray for spring to come soon.

Myriad thoughts come to you as you lie awake on a sleepless night, further dashing all hopes of sleep away. The ticking of a clock can be your only companion as you hope that either sleep will descend or morning shall dawn so that the excuse of sleeping could end.

A simple poem about a simple situation in life.

SLEEPLESSNESS

It's winter still....the cold air doth blow
All that was life is now covered with snow
And I lie here alone and yet awake
Living through this winter for its own sake

If only spring would come and spread its bliss
O'er the frosty helplessness this cold is
May mountains shine again with sparkling day
May my heart again beat all pain away

I have but no reason to be awake
But am counting the minutes to daybreak
The ticking of the clock tells me I live
The world cares not, neither forgets nor forgives

The winter is long, the night grows cold
In these endless hours...may my day unfold.

Jim Morrison, the American poet better known as the lead singer of the band 'The Doors', has written some amazing poetry. He was a beat poet when the world was just waking up to the genre. Regrettably Jim died too soon, and the world was deprived of much of his greatness. His poem 'Awake', a true awakening from a state of insobriety to the 'day's divinity', asks what is the 'first thing you see?'

Do you see the beauty of being alive, young, lovely, filled with vigour? Or do you see the self-same drunkenness and stoned state of despair, where there is no hope, where 'everything is broken up and dances'?

Jim Morrison created elusively surreal images in the poem, of the 'Sweet Forest' and the 'Hot Dream'. I have taken his poem and tried to carve an answer to him in his own language.

Since it's my first attempt at writing a 'beat poem', I could only do it with the 'Curses, Invocations' of the beat poet himself.

AWAKE

I am awake today, shaking my hair
And do you dare question my wakefulness?
No sweet child am I and no pretty one
I have chosen the day, it's just begun

I see the vast radiant beach with jewelled moon
Couples naked race, we smugly do swoon
Mad children caught in woolly infancy
Crooning ancient ones to divinity

All that is broken up and still dances
Finds the radiant moon yet prances
Beside the ancient lake and sweet forest
May you enter the hot dream and still find rest

Beneath the moon, beside the ancient lake
From forests of hot dreams I am awake.

We all have them. Their magnitude may differ, we deal with them every day, but do we have what it takes to face them? People panic when a problem comes, it is so easy to blame others when things go wrong, subordinates, colleagues anyone who can take the blame away from us while we ostrich-like hide and hope that it shall pass.

I heard it once, 'a strong man is not he who can hit the weak, a man is he who can drink the poison with the nectar and still stand.'...a true calling of manhood... Or womanhood for that matter...do we have what it takes to stand and take the blame, with no eye on the problem but on the solution...because delving on the problem will not solve...but as soon as a problem happens to delve on the solution is something that not many of us can do.

So how do you want to solve a problem? By hiding? By blaming? Or by facing it with a solution? The choice is yours.

PROBLEM

With a door knock, with a bell ring they come
Letters, calls from the boss, and you succumb
Worries surround and a wreck you become
End of joy is the start of a problem

Can you face it? Do you have the clout
To take the blows during this tricky bout?
Will you stand aside and just bite your nail?
When the ostrich like tactic too might fail.

Or will you take it head on with poise and grace
With no concern for the problem that you face
With eye on the solution and nothing more
That resolves any problem, opens any door

Have faith in you alone when things go wrong
Problems and solutions do ride along.

This is the prayer of a penitent man...who is praying for redemption...but the sinful world still surrounds...can he be rid of it? Torn apart from the right and the wrong...that is how we live in the world...guilt remains and hope for salvation...whether one gets it may depend on the degree of supplication.

SUPPLICATION

I bow to you dear Lord with folded hands,
Hoping for release from all these strands,
That bind me to these erring worldly needs,
That leaves me wanting and yet succeeds

In keeping me wanting still, greed prevails,
It does not leave me, and it does not fail
To keep me away from You and I feel
Remorse! for who I am, that's why I kneel.

I am a sinner Lord and yet You grace
Me with joy of life and health, embrace
Me with Love even though I am nothing,
But a mortal who awaits your coming.

Dear Lord hear my earnest supplication
May my prayer be your resurrection.

Written as a response to John Lennon's cult song 'Imagine'—a song that enthused the beat generation of the '70s—does it have any relevance today? This is the question discussed in these further Sonnets of Opposites.

The first of these being a tearing down of the utopia Lennon created. The world that then swung with hope as the song played on. 'Imagine' a thousand Zippo lighters lit up as the song was being sung. That was the mood 'Imagine' created and maybe it still does.

But the world did not change, all that was imagined to be 'no more', exists still, no lessons have been learnt. The world is still torn apart by nations that fight for supremacy, greed and hunger wrecks the peace that Lennon hoped to feel. There is no peace...anywhere.

Unity is but a far cry, when there is still just too much to hate for. The world is not the 'one' that was 'imagined', it is still very far from it.

So why imagine at all? Imagination is dead!

IMAGINE DEAD

It's an 'Ancient Dream' today...meaningless
Easy no more... Hell is! we are sky less
Imagining a heaven still, no doubt
Yet tomorrow's what our today's all about

Countries are not what divide us no more
People, ideas. Faiths, divide cities too
Nothing compares to life's fears anymore
All strangers are feared now, all door knocks too

Does the utopia exist anywhere?
Will imagining serve any purpose
Can we hope to dream? Can we even dare?
Brotherhood of man is but a carcass

Long gone you are, and yes the only one
An ancient song that remains unsung

My tribute to John Lennon's cause, the revolution does not stop, never can, there will always be people hoping to make the world a better place. Many things that Lennon imagined are already a reality. New hopes of utopia exist today, which if finds the right following, as it has already, in another generation, with a younger, more determined blood. 'Imagine' will be alive again.

IMAGINE AGAIN

Dear John, we take it from where you left
Imagining, the world's yet not bereft
Of dreamers, no acid rain, no global warming
No terror strikes, or killer bombings

People leaving home in peace, returning too
Not mugged in an alley, nor pink slipped too
Not stuck in traffic for hours at end
People finding true love and also a friend

No dictators, and no school massacres
No thirst for want of clean water and rain
No corrupt politics, no feared hackers
No greed or hunger, brotherhood regained

Others have joined, you're not the only one
Imagining perfection has just begun

'We don't need no Education!' is what the song 'Another Brick in the Wall' was all about. A boy had given me the word 'Floyd' so naturally the first thought that came to me was the song. For the song is the best-known work by Pink Floyd, the band. As a teacher I cannot help being pedantic. So this poem talks about keeping kids in school, a little lesson in the need for education.

Education can never go waste. As arrogant teenagers, sometimes they feel that they are beyond education and coming to school is just a waste of time. But my advice to them is, stay in school, complete school education with good marks, many doors will be open to you once you have the School Pass Certificate. It will be handy to you all your life.

Even if your ambition lies in fields that don't really require school education, still school is a must for every child. The path you choose after school is really upto you, but do stay on in school.

YOU ARE THE BRICK IN THE WALL
(Part 1)

I have seen you, moping the corridors
Unsure, sceptical, whether you belong
You feel you don't need to be in school, these doors
Cloister you from the fresh air that you long

Who stops you? go on! live free! do you need
These prison walls that capture you?
You can go when you want, just please concede...
There's more to know than what think you do,

Your first words were written here, A B C
Your best friends are still here, don't you agree?
Those who saw you through thick and thin
Are waiting here still for your life to begin

It's just another brick in the wall I know
It's up to you to make it strong or weak though

When I showed the Part 1 to my friend Ahmed, his first thought was that it was too pro-norm, sort of me saying what I was expected to say as a teacher. This led to my writing another in the series of Sonnets of Opposites. Not really an 'opposing' thought to part 1, but still a different form of advice to the young.

If you have the courage, break the barriers that bind you, school and education is not stopping you from conquering your dream, education is not the road block to your ambition. Mindsets maybe, but you can pave your own way, if the way is blocked by any sort of wall. Elders stopping you in your path, society, school etc. You will have to break the wall, not by violence, not by arrogance, but by putting your case forward most convincingly.

Break the wall of misunderstanding, that will be a rebellion worth winning, not only for you, who knows if you can carve a new way for yourself, it may be a path that others too can take, following you, a new leader!!

BREAK THE BRICK IN THE WALL
(Part 2)

We don't need no education! you say
Fine pave it and you find a new way
If it be real you will find followers
From many of life's shades, many colours

The wall's the thing, it's not education
That's keeping you closed, leave hesitation
And break the damn wall and leave it all still!
Make a mountain from the very molehill

Because you can and it's so in your power
This is your time, this your very hour
To take on where the others have left
Revolution of martyrs is never bereft

Barriers cannot restrain free will that's passed
Revolution's dream shall the wall so blast

A simple sonnet, for my soulmate, my wife. It's a blessing to find one's soulmate in one's life, I am blessed to have found mine.

My prayer for all readers is that you too may find your soulmate, but not only find the love, but honour and respect that love. Because love is eternal yes! But love needs to be renewed and worked on day after day. So love well and live well too!

SOULMATE

I knew it from the first time that we met
When we completed each other's sentences
We said the same things all the time and yet
Had our own minds and our differences

We both love the same things with time we knew
As life took us forward, love did so too
In between it all we realized also
That we're in love, that's what matters more

I see us growing old together
Sitting side by side no matter the weather
In dark nights bleak and oh so scary
And on summer days so hot and weary

My soulmate when our very souls are one
Our foreverness has only just begun.

I was given this word by my friend Sanjay Sane. It is definitely a complex thought and required a complex poem. So it may be confusing at first, the reader may need to read it again to get the meaning.

It should have happened to every reader, when a moment occurs that you feel has happened before... Call it rebirth if you must, in which some say we must go through similar life experiences to learn from them till we get them right. Call it déjà vu, where in the same life time we have the same experiences, again, to resolve something unresolved. It could simply be a scientific chemical reaction in the brain, when you just feel all this has happened before but is just a reaction happening in the body. Or it could be a fabrication of one's subconscious that occurs and one's feels that déjà vu happens.

Whatever be the reality of déjà vu, it is an interesting yet a confusing experience... May we live and learn.

DÉJÀ VU

I have been here and am here again
What was, is here, and yet could it remain?
Wanting itself to be new is not to be,
What was, is again, but soon 'was' will be

Is the past yet to happen? Is that real?
Or is the real happening so surreal?
That we don't realize the now from the then
When the time past seems to happen again

Have we lived it all? is the now a dream?
The reality of which just does seem
Surreal but is the experience whence
What has been done, will be done again, hence

Every time déjà vu may happen though,
We do anew that we have done before.

It's a question of evolution and existence, Darwin himself said that 'Evolution' is the survival of the fittest. Definitely it has connotations that a fight must happen and the 'fittest' will survive.

How different is Darwin then from every other historian? Whoever has written history is as per the version of the victor. All those who win wars become the heroes and history is written with them as the 'Good guys', is that the correct history then?

Is that is what is evolution? Then it too is questionable, if the only way for history to move forward is by them who survive in the fight for existence...by those who are the fittest... Are we still not but the cavemen that we were? Or like the dinosaurs hunting for our prey? Have education, the holy books, the lives of Buddha, Christ, Gandhi not taught us anything? If it is only the fittest who will survive, does the path of non-violence have any meaning? Or is it that non-violence is the 'fittest' way forward?

Evolution poses so many questions, maybe a poem alone cannot answer.

EVOLUTION

Darwin's theory had the world so amazed
That the world spins to results so crazed
In a fraction we—the unfit, could be
A statistic, a point in history.

Like the dinosaurs, or even the big bang
Ere the world around us even began
Are we just marks in the sands of time?
Is there any reason or any rhyme?

For our existence, the fit shall live on...
For them there's no doubt the past is long gone
But who is the fit? Who is there to say?
Do we have to fight for it, every day?

Tell me have we ev'n begun to evolve?
When fighting for 'existence' isn't resolved.

'What a piece of work is man?' Shakepeare asked this wonderful question, talked of here as God's masterpiece. From a Christian perspective no doubt, but the excellent piece of work man is, getting better and better in intelligence and thought with every generation. We are actually becoming God-like in our intellect, evolution makes us perfect. The masterpiece just keeps getting better.

MASTERPIECE

We are works of passion, we're someone's dream
Made not in a moment as the book might deem
With ages of thought of how the best will be
Perfection is no swap for mediocrity

We are perfect, see your hands, your torso
Your face in the mirror, expression aglow
Eyes with unsurpassing splendour and gleam
Voices with the sounds of angels may seem

Mind that evolves and creates even more
Opening shut ideas, opening closed doors
Ideas can change the world from war to peace
We humans are God's one such masterpiece

We make us beyond all God's creation
Perfect in the twirl of evolution

A contentment in the lap of nature, a simple word, with a simple message of contentment makes up the first of another of the 'Sonnets about Opposites'. The setting could be anywhere in the beautiful wildernesses that the world has to offer, the reader can imagine one's own beautiful place that brings contentment. Just feel content at being alive and well and happy, that is all.

CONTENT

Sitting on this rock at the peak of this mount
I see the valley and this lovely lake
Green with envy as the peaks do taunt
Serenity does this moment pious make

It's all quiet here, and the breeze does blow
With forgiveness of all the airs below
That tried to make this moment unquiet indeed
Awaiting divinity to succeed

It's a moment to be held in the palm
No malice yet can succumb to the grace
Of this minute on hills run wild with calm
As we find meaning in all that we face

We are content with the love of nature
May this same love transcend to all creatures.

But sitting at the peak, one can see below, at all the ugliness there is. The surroundings cannot hide how terrible the world has become. And there is nothing one can do from up there but be an objective spectator. Which is really how many of us live our lives...considering ourselves 'above' the ugliness, and talk about it in condescending ways. Maybe one should get down from the pinnacle and do something real about it, rather than just continue to 'boil' at the situation the world is in.

DISCONTENT

Sitting at the peak is not a respite
From all the ugliness below and spite
It is more clear when one sits way up here
Rottenness of the world plainly appears

Up here one just hopes for peace and quiet
Cannot have it when the world's a riot
Created by self-serving leaders of men
Who rape the world again and again

If only I had the might of this peak
To draw out the splendour with its light
And shun the darkness for the shine I seek
In this anguish of discontent, find respite

Yet the world below revels in turmoil
And discontent at the chaos doth boil

Written for the word of a child who has just passed out of school and who has shown so much promise while in school, now that the real world beckons, there is much to achieve, much to do.

My advice to such a child would have to be, do not settle for mediocrity, but be willing to work for the best...because you can...

Whatever drives you is secondary, is it money? Fine... Is it fame? All the better... But ensure that everyday adds something more to your esteem.

There is a lesson I have learnt from my mother. She would say at the end of a year I would look back and see through the year, what I have achieved...and thankfully through every year... I had something more in my life...that is progress... Stagnation is an easy lane to fall into, the quiet, unopposing path when all may seem quiet and nothing further required to work for...but will then lead you to a way where you may find yourselves years after at the same place.

So go with the fast lane...it will have many road blocks, many detours too, but the journey will be eventful and will definitely take you to new destinations of progress.

PROGRESS

I wake every day with the same promise
That today I shall add more to my life
It's not easy to do when the climb is
So filled with struggle and with so much strife

But yet each day I do manage to fill
My day with some value added to me
That does make me so indispensable
And adds value to the worth of me

Yet it's not enough!... I seek the stars
And that's where I see me in years to be
Not what is now or where my now hours are
But where dreams say I'm supposed to be

I know I have miles to go as of yet
Progress's ladder is still to be set

Who is the showman here? Christ himself... He came to this world to establish the kingdom of God... How could he do it for people who were uneducated and village folk. Christ had to show miracles, bring the dead to life, heal the lame and the blind and drive spirits away. Only then would they follow him. To make things simple all He did was tell stories, called parables in the Bible.

Christ made his ministry as simple as possible, adding to it the showmanship that was so required. How else would He get an audience of five thousand people and then feed them? This was again the act of a showman.

His death again must have been an amazing show, for those who believed and those who did not know, seeing a man flogged and wearing a crown of thorns, carrying a cross of over 120 kilograms. For nearly a kilometer, and then to be nailed to it, must have been quite an amazing show.

Did Christ need to put up such a show? Probably He did for the non-believer... Probably He did not...for a believer... I can say that now, but probably I too need that whole show to believe. Without that show...who would bother with this child who was born in a manger and claimed to be the son of God. A man who might have done some amazing things but just died in some unamazing way. It all had to be spectacular for us to believe and so it was.

He was a showman that we needed, to be the eternal superstar that He is.

SHOWMAN

They thronged in scores, in thousands behind him
Why did they? Was it all just for the show?
Where were the multitudes when he was whipped
From the base of the cross, where did they go?

They were hurling abuses as he walked
Burdened not just by the heavy piece of wood
Another show being played for those who stalked
The showman at his work, yet none understood

Again today we see these acts played out
Again people throng for miracle shows
Faith in mighty healings is all its about
But what faith is? does no one really know?

Do we need miracles to know it's Him?
Show is not salvation, but faith within.

ACKNOWLEDGEMENTS

My sincere thanks to everyone who has given me their words. I cannot take credit for the words given to me, it is therefore a combined effort that is presented here. I also wish to thank my friends for their inputs and kind words of encouragement. I also thank my mother and sister who made me the person who I am and gave me the power to be perceptive and determined to hope and to dream. I thank Avish, my young nephew, who has been my first reader and critic. Most of all to my wife Shweta for her patience with me and for going through each poem again and again, telling me what I can do to improve each one, proofreading this manuscript for me over and over. She has been my pillar of strength and the drive behind this endeavour.

I also thank all my teachers and the great poets who have gone before, because of them I attempt to write something new from the literature that I was taught, the basis upon which I hope to keep poetry alive in a new era. But whether I have succeeded in doing so is really up to the readers. My final thanks therefore is to you, dear reader, to have read this manuscript. I hope you have read through the poems and found 'something' to carry away with you from the pages of these Sonnets about Nothing.

God Bless!

Made in the USA
Middletown, DE
24 May 2020